Published by Creative Education
123 South Broad Street, Mankato, Minnesota 56001
Creative Education is an imprint of The Creative Company

Designed by Stephanie Blumenthal
Production Design by The Design Lab
Editorial Assistance by Julie Bach

Photos by: AP/Wide World Photos, Arkansas Democrat Gazette,
FPG International, Globe Photos, Oxford University, PhotoDisc Inc.,
Retna Ltd., Reuters/Corbis-Bettmann, Rex USA Ltd., Shooting Star,
Time Warner, Washington Photos, Wellesley College

Library of Congress Cataloging-in-Publication Data

Loewen, Nancy.
Hillary Rodham Clinton / by Nancy Loewen
p. cm. – (Ovations)
Summary: Describes the life of the First Lady of the United States
from her youth to her current career.
ISBN 0-88682-636-5

1. Clinton, Hillary Rodham–Juvenile literature. 2. Presidents' spouses–
United States–Biography–Juvenile literature. [1. Clinton, Hillary Rodham
2. First ladies.] I. Title. II. Series: Ovations (Mankato, Minn.)

E887.C55L64   1999
973.929'092–dc21   97-50795

First edition

2 4 6 8 9 7 5 3 1

HILLARY RODHAM

CLINTON

BY NANCY LOEWEN

Creative 🍎 Education

REFLECTIONS

Three thousand people packed into a movie theater in Huairou, China, north of Beijing. Thousands more stood in the rain outside. They were delegates attending the 1995 United Nations Conference on Women. And they were all waiting to hear one of the keynote speakers, Hillary Rodham Clinton.

Hillary stepped onto the stage and began her speech. In it, she criticized Chinese leaders who had prevented large numbers of women from attending the conference. "Freedom means the right of people to assemble, organize, and debate openly," she said. "It means respecting the views of those who may disagree with the views of their governments."

Her speech continued. In it she emphasized her belief that women everywhere should be allowed basic human rights.

Her speech and her attendance at the conference caused much controversy. Some people said that her speech was too critical of the Chinese government. Some praised it for bringing up issues that others won't talk about. Some thought she shouldn't have attended the conference at all.

People have strong opinions about Hillary Rodham Clinton. To many she is a symbol of much that is wrong with the world—a world in which the traditional family structure has fallen away in favor of two parents working outside the home.

To many she is a symbol of much that is right with the world—a world in which women and minorities increasingly participate in decisions that shape our society.

Public life includes many speaking engagements. Hillary Rodham Clinton shook hands with members of the League of Women Voters in 1994, before addressing them about health care.

EVOLUTION

Hillary Diane Rodham was born in Chicago on October 26, 1947, and grew up in the conservative, tree-lined suburban community of Park Ridge, Illinois. Her father, Hugh, owned a small textile business, and her mother, Dorothy, was a homemaker. Hillary had two younger brothers, Hugh Jr. and Tony.

From an early age, Hillary stood out as an achiever, earning all the badges as a Brownie and Girl Scout; playing softball, volleyball, and other sports; and taking piano and ballet lessons. Her parents encouraged and supported her efforts, but they were also firm disciplinarians. "I didn't run afoul of my parents very often," Hillary said. "They were strict about my respecting authority, and not just parental authority. My father's favorite saying was: 'You get in trouble at

school, you get in trouble at home.'"

Her family's church, too, was an important influence. The Rodhams attended the First Methodist Church, and Hillary was active in the youth group. One of the group's ongoing projects was helping the children of local migrant workers. This experience and others like it helped instill in Hillary a sense of social responsibility. "What my church taught me," she said, "is, because I had those blessings from that family, I owed something back."

In high school Hillary was friendly and well liked—and always very busy. She was a member of the National Honor Society and served as vice president of the junior class. She graduated in the top five percent of her class. Not surprisingly, the other seniors voted Hillary Rodham most likely to succeed.

Beginning in the fall of 1965, Hillary attended Wellesley College in Massachusetts, majoring in political science. At that time a cultural revolution was taking place. Young people were making their voices heard on the Vietnam War and the Civil Rights Movement. Hillary reveled in the college atmosphere—long, earnest political discussions with friends; late-night study sessions; dancing to the Beatles and the Supremes. Her political affiliation gradually shifted from Republican, which her parents were, to Democrat.

In college, Hillary was a popular and active student. As a senior, she served as government president at Wellesley.

Popular and outgoing, Hillary was widely respected for her intelligence as well as her leadership abilities. In her senior year she served as president of the college government and got a taste of celebrity status when she put in an impressive appearance on the popular TV quiz show "College Bowl." She received even more attention at her graduation. As class speaker she raised eyebrows and caused a few gasps when she bluntly rebuked the speaker who preceded her, a Massachusetts senator, for "irrelevant thinking." The event made *Life* magazine, which included her picture and an excerpt from her speech.

After graduating from Wellesley, Hillary attended Yale Law School, where she was one of only thirty women in her class. At Yale she met Bill Clinton, an earnest and intelligent student from Arkansas, and the two liked each other immediately. "I learned quickly that he was unlike anybody I'd ever met—and still is," Hillary explained in 1993, "because he combined an absolutely extraordinary mind with a huge heart. It is just not that usual to find people with both those great gifts. And we just started talking and never stopped, I guess is the best way to say it. We are still talking."

Both Hillary and Bill were interested in using the law as a means to contribute to society. "Everyone [at Yale] was ambitious," a classmate recalled. "But I see Bill and Hillary as driven by almost a religious purpose of some sort. They had the sort of late sixties sense of *we have to make the world better.* Not 'I have to make the world better,' but 'we,' all people, acting together."

During one summer between semesters, Hillary moved to Washington, D.C., to work for the Washington Research Project. Part of her work was to study the conditions of migrant workers and their children in labor camps. The experience reinforced her interest in children's issues. She stayed an extra year at Yale to study children's legal theory.

At that point, Bill had a much clearer sense of direction than Hillary did. He wanted to return to Arkansas and do good for his people. Few people on campus could relate to such a quest. Arkansas was beset with many problems, including poverty, racism, and a deteriorating education system. Hillary knew that if she continued to date Bill, she would almost certainly have to move to Arkansas. She wasn't sure she wanted to.

After graduating from Yale Law School in 1973, Hillary took a job as a staff attorney for the Children's Defense Fund in Cambridge, Massachusetts. Within a few months, however, the 26-year-old lawyer was asked to serve on the Watergate legal team, a nonpartisan committee charged with investigating allegations of misconduct by President Richard Nixon. The hours were long and the work was intense, but Hillary felt it was exciting to be a part of history. "She was very much a team player, with absolutely no sense of prima donna about her," a colleague recalled. "She was particularly sensitive to other people when they were down. She was really a very supportive person."

When Nixon resigned in August 1974 and the committee disbanded, Hillary was faced with a decision. Should she go back to her job with the Children's Defense Fund? Should she take one of the high-profile, high-paying jobs that were being offered to her? Or should she join Bill in Arkansas?

The couple had now been apart for nearly a year. While Hillary had worked in Massachusetts, Bill had been teaching law at the University of Arkansas in Fayetteville and preparing to run for Congress. Hillary decided

Issues dealing with education and children are of particular importance to Hillary, and she sometimes visits schools to bring the issues into the news.

SAFEWAY
SUPPORTS
AFFORDABLE
HEALTH CARE
for all
AMERICANS.

to follow her heart. She moved to Fayetteville, took a teaching job, and became Bill's campaign manager in his first bid for public office. Although Bill lost the election, he received a higher percentage of votes than any other Democratic candidate ever had in that district. It seemed clear that he was a rising political star.

After the election, the two were married on October 11, 1975. They had a small ceremony in the modest brick house that Bill had bought two months earlier. "It was the simplest ceremony possible, but also the most beautiful," remembered Hillary's mother.

DEFENDING HER GOALS

The next year, Bill Clinton was elected attorney general and the couple moved to Little Rock; two years later he was elected governor. In 1977 Hillary began practicing law at the highly regarded Rose Law Firm. She advanced to partner a few years later, becoming one of the first women in the state to join a major firm. She served as a founding member and president of the state's first advocacy group, the Arkansas Advocates for Children and Families. And she was chair of a committee to deliver health care to isolated communities.

In addition to her roles as political wife and lawyer, she soon had another role to play: that of mother. Chelsea Clinton was born on February 27, 1980.

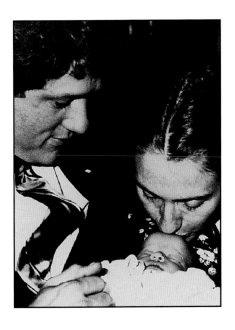

During Bill's terms in the Arkansas state government, Hillary practiced at the Rose Law Firm. It was at this time that the couple celebrated the birth of their daughter Chelsea.

That year was a difficult one, however. Bill Clinton lost his bid for reelection as governor. There were several reasons for his defeat, and, unfortunately, Hillary was one of them. She was different from most political wives, and many voters were put off by her behavior. Besides continuing to work at her own career, she had also kept her own last name. Arkansas didn't seem to be ready for such an independent first lady.

The family moved out of the governor's mansion, and Bill took a position with a law firm. But two years later he hit the campaign trail for governor once again, and Hillary was right beside him. Realizing that she would have to make some changes if she wanted her message to be heard, she began using the name Mrs. Bill Clinton in social situations. At the same time, she inspired people with her impassioned public speaking. In good part because of Hillary's efforts, Bill was reelected governor and the family moved back into the governor's mansion, where they remained for the next ten years.

The Clintons have been together through many political battles since meeting at Yale Law School—wins, losses, and emotional decisions. In 1988, opposite, Bill decided against running for president.

One of Hillary's greatest achievements in Arkansas came as chair of the Arkansas Education Standards Committee, to which she was appointed in 1983. At that time, Arkansas students were scoring far below national averages in math and reading, and the entire system—from administrators to teachers to kids—seemed to not care. Hillary helped bring about needed changes such as reduced classroom size and teacher testing. Other states copied the successful program. She also helped develop a program to help parents prepare their children for school.

With Hillary as his adviser and top supporter, Bill Clinton's political ambition grew. In 1988 he wanted to run for president, but after much consideration, he decided against it. He and Hillary were concerned about spending too much time away from seven-year-old Chelsea. They also didn't want to expose her to the political mudslinging that would likely take place. Four years later, however, the entire family rose to the challenge as Bill Clinton declared himself a candidate for the presidency of the United States.

In many respects, Hillary was the backbone of the 1992 Clinton campaign. Bill himself admitted that she was "far better organized, more in control, more intelligent and more eloquent" than he was. But while many people applauded her efforts and wondered why she wasn't running for office herself, others disliked her, much as they had in the Arkansas governor's race in 1980. Trying to defend herself in the course of the grueling campaign, Hillary unintentionally added fuel to the fire with the statements: "I'm not some little woman standing by her man like Tammy Wynette" and "I suppose I could have stayed home and baked cookies and had teas, but what I decided to do is fulfill my profession." Many women felt Hillary had insulted them.

Hillary found this reaction frustrating and painful. She was not, as one writer said, "a radical feminist who has little use for religious values or even the traditional family unit." Rather, she supported the right of all people to pursue their dreams. In an address to a women's business organization, she said that she would fight the effort to label her as either a careerist or a wife and mother. "I am all of those things and I am more than the sum of the parts: I am me," she stated. "I will continue to refuse the kind of stereotyping that tries to strip from me or tries to strip from anyone your individual dignity and your identity, because what I want . . . is a community where we celebrate one another and recognize the complexity of who we are."

With her help and support during campaigns, Bill Clinton was elected President of the United States in 1992 and again in 1996. Her role as First Lady has allowed her to bring issues such as education and health care to the stage for national debate.

Despite many obstacles, in November 1992 Bill Clinton was elected president of the United States. The day after the election was a dream fulfilled. "I woke up," President Clinton recalled. "She looked at me, and I looked at her, and we just started laughing, like, 'Can you believe that this happened to us?' "

A VOICE FOR OTHERS

Hillary Rodham Clinton brought her energies to the role of the nation's First Lady. In her first six months at the White House she headed a 500-member task force on health care reform. The illness and death of her father, who suffered a severe stroke in March and died in April 1993, added to the pressure, and at the same time made her job more personally meaningful.

Hillary's work on the health care reform task force proved to be difficult and controversial. Many Americans resented her high-profile position, pointing out that Bill, not Hillary, had been elected by the voters.

Others praised her efforts and were grateful for a passionate advocate for women and children at the head of such an important committee.

When the task force's recommendations were not passed into law, Hillary accepted the defeat and moved on. In order to quiet mounting criticism from the media, she chose to downplay her role as adviser at the White House for a while.

In 1996, American voters reelected Bill Clinton. After the inauguration, Hillary made clear her plans to fight for women's rights around the world and to champion the needs of children. In 1995 she spoke at the United Nations Conference on Women in Beijing, China. Then, in 1996, her book, *It Takes a Village And Other Lessons Children Teach Us*, was published. In the book she encourages parents, teachers, government officials, and all Americans to support children in our society and help them grow into healthy, able, resilient adults.

Hillary also enjoys aspects of the traditional role of the First Lady. She entertains guests with grace and dignity. She also spends time with Chelsea. When Chelsea was in grade school and high school, Hillary helped

Hillary won a Grammy Award for the spoken word version of her book, It Takes A Village And Other Lessons Children Teach Us.

with homework and attended school functions. The two also traveled together. In 1996, they visited six African countries as ambassadors of good will and advocates for women's and children's rights.

Bill Clinton's second term as president has been plagued by scandals, some of which involve Hillary. The media's harassment and constant questioning keep her from doing the work she loves to do: helping people live healthier, more fulfilling lives. Hillary's code is simple: We are all here to help someone else. "She believes that to the core of her being," one of her top aides said.

Not everyone in America is happy with the prominent role Hillary has in matters of policy; she is not an elected official, after all. But as the president said, "I think she can easily do what she's supposed to do as First Lady and still have time and energy to be involved in some of these specific areas. . . . I would be derelict in my duty to the United States if I did not use her."

No matter how long she remains in the White House or what project she takes on, Hillary Rodham Clinton is undoubtedly among the most powerful women in history. She is a force for change in our world.

Political service to the United States government involves visiting other countries. Below, Hillary and Chelsea spoke with Pakistani Prime Minister Benazir Bhutto and her son in 1995.

VOICES

ON LIFE IN THE
WHITE HOUSE:

"I keep saying to the people here,
'You know the kind of macaroni we
like comes in a yellow and red box,'
and they look at me like I'm from
another planet. I've got to buy it and
show it to them."

Hillary Rodham Clinton

"A speech that needs a rewrite, get
Hillary. A speech that needs to be
given, get Hillary. The President has
a problem he wants to chew over, get
Hillary. The point is you never go
wrong in getting Hillary."

White House aide

ON HER PERSONALITY:

"I've never seen her lose her temper, and you can tell her anything."
  Paula Begala, White House political consultant

"I'm efficient, and she makes me look like a daydreamer."
  Melanne Verveer, deputy to Hillary Rodham Clinton

ON HER MESSAGE TO THE AMERICAN PEOPLE:

"Make a pact not to give in to selfishness or cynicism or hate. Cling to the enduring values you have been exposed to. Cling especially to the value that is given to all people and that is premised on their equal worth. Respect and trust individuals of all races, creeds, and colors. Work toward the achievement of a universal human dignity, not just your own personal security."

Hillary Rodham Clinton

One of Hillary's major concerns is health care reform. She attends benefits for causes such as Alzheimer's research, and she speaks before councils and committees on the need to make affordable health care a priority.

"I think the greatest gift you can give children is to help them develop self-respect and the skills valuable to them, so they can be the people God meant them to be."

Hillary Rodham Clinton

"If there ever was an idea that [women] could be ignored, there certainly can no longer be."

Hillary Rodham Clinton

Volunteerism is an issue that the Clintons promote; above, they served Thanksgiving dinner at the Blair Shelter in Washington.

"I've always believed you play the hand you're dealt, and you play it as well as you can. You take every precaution you possibly can to make sure that, at the end of the day, you are glad you lived it that way, and you know that you did the best job you could do."

Hillary Rodham Clinton

"The good days far outweigh the bad days. Sure, there are times you can get down, but boy, when the high occur, they are like nothing else."

Hillary Rodham Clinton

As First Lady, Hillary has had to wear many hats—professional, political, and social. She accompanied Bill to Oxford where he received an honorary civil law degree, left; she joined him at the Democratic convention, below; and she visited a magnet school for students interested in medical careers, opposite, to promote her health care reform plan.

On the Future:

"I want to travel around and talk to people about what is happening on the ground. I intend to speak out about it and write about it."

Hillary Rodham Clinton

"I think we upset a lot of people because we are encouraging change, and change is frightening to many. But I have no doubts we are on the right track."

Hillary Rodham Clinton

Supporters and critics alike agree that Hillary Rodham Clinton has made an impact on the U.S. and has changed the role of the First Lady for times to come.

OVATIONS